What Do We Know About Sound?

Close your eyes and sit quietly for a few moments. You will hear many different sounds. The sounds that enter our ears are all made by something. That 'something' is the sound **source**.

📖 **1a List the sounds you can hear.**
📖 **1b What made these sounds?**

Look at the pictures.

2 Which of these sounds do you like best? Why?

3 Which of these sounds do you like least? Why?

The sound source is not usually right next to your ears but you can still hear the sound it makes.

📖 **4 How do you think you can hear sounds from a sound source that is *not* next to you?**

Science Skills

Classify it!

There are many different types of sounds. We find some much nicer to listen to than others. We sometimes call unpleasant sounds **noise**.

Word box

high
loud
low
noise
quiet
volume

1 Talk to a partner. What types of sound would you describe as noise?

A fire alarm

A dog barking

A flute being played

Sounds can be different **volumes**. The volume is how **loud** or **quiet** a sound is. Some sounds can easily be heard. These are loud sounds. Others are much more difficult to hear because they are quiet.

Guitar music

2a When do you use a loud voice?
2b When do you use a quiet voice?

A whistle

A bird singing

A hand bell

Someone singing

We can sort sounds in different ways.

3a In a group, describe the different sounds made by the things in the diagrams on these pages.

3b Name one of the things that makes a **high** sound.

3c Name one of the things that makes a **low** sound.

4 Find two different ways of sorting the sounds made by these eight sound sources.

Making Sounds

Musical instruments

Making sounds using instruments

You will need some instruments like the ones in the diagram.

1 Work in a group and use the instruments to make sounds.

2 Discuss how the sounds were made.

Sounds are made because something is **vibrating**. Vibrating means moving backwards and forwards very quickly. Sometimes these vibrations are easy to see, like the strings on a guitar. Sometimes these vibrations are not as easy to see, like when a whistle is blown.

1 What vibrates to make sound on each type of musical instrument you used?

Vibrating Air

We know when bees are flying close to us because of the buzzing sound they make. Bees flap their wings very quickly when they move. This makes the air around them vibrate. The vibrations of the wings and the air make the buzzing sound.

1 Find out how we can hear hummingbirds hum.

2 List three other animals that make sounds as they move and explain how the sounds are made.

3 Why is it important for some animals to move very quietly?

When the guitar string is plucked it vibrates. This movement makes the air next to the string vibrate too. The air passes the vibrations to our ears and then we hear the sound.

4 Explain how we hear a whistle when it is blown.

Explaining How We Hear

To hear sounds from the sound source we need vibrations to pass from the air to our ears. First they reach the **outer ear** and then go inside the ear until they reach the **auditory nerve**, where the vibrations are turned into signals that are sent to the brain.

Word box
auditory nerve
outer ear

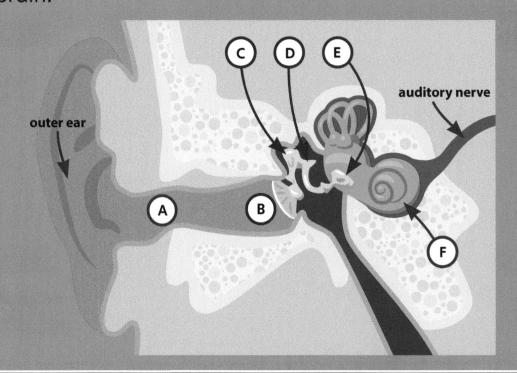

outer ear

auditory nerve

C   D   E

A   B   F

Look closely at this diagram of the parts inside our ears.

Find out what the different parts are called and how they transmit the sound.

📄 1 Label the parts of the ear.

📄 2 Research and explain how sound is transmitted from the outer ear to the brain.

Modelling How Sound Travels

Scientists use models to help them explain how different phenomena occur. A **phenomenon** is something we can observe as it happens but we cannot see how it is happening.

Sound is a phenomenon as we can hear the vibrations when they reach our ear, but we cannot see how they get to our ears.

Sound travels through the air as **compression waves**. We can use a 'slinky' spring as a model to help us understand these sound waves.

Slinky model

You will need: a slinky spring

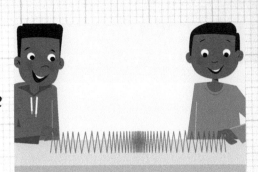

1 Work in a pair and stretch the slinky spring out like the one in the diagram.

2 Hold one end still.

3 Move the other end of the slinky quickly towards and away from the other end of the slinky by about 10 cm several times.

4 Observe what happens along the length of the slinky.

This is a model for a sound wave.

Predict it!

Sound travels to reach our ears. If you close the door and window in your bedroom you can usually still hear some sounds from outside the room.

1a Which sounds can you sometimes hear from outside when your classroom door and windows are closed?

1b How do you hear sounds from sound sources that are outside the room?

can sound travel through solids?

work in a small group. You will need samples of the materials in the diagram that are larger than your hand.

1 Do you think sound will travel through each of these solids?

2 Place the sample on your table and put your ear on it. Tap the sample with your finger.

3 Does the sound travel through the material?

Sound Travels Through Liquids

When we put our ears under water we can still hear sounds.

1a Have you ever swum under water? What could you hear?

1b Did the sounds sound the same as when you were out of the water?

Comparing solid, liquid and gas

Work in a small group. You will need: 3 identical plastic boxes with lids, water, sand

1 Fill one box with water, another with sand and leave air in the third. Put the lids on tightly.

2 Place them on the table. Put your ear next to each box in turn and tap it with your finger.

3 What happens to the sound of the tapping each time?

4 Does sound travel through the solid, liquid and gas? How do you know?

Changing Pitch

Every sound has a **frequency**. The frequency is the number of vibrations in one second. This determines how high or low a sound is. We call this the **pitch** of the sound. A high sound is squeaky like a mouse. A low sound is deep like the bark of a big dog.

Word box

frequency
pitch

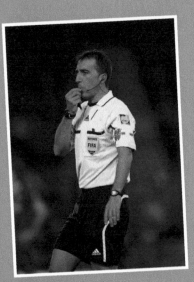

A referee's whistle makes very fast vibrations so it produces many vibrations in a second and a very high-pitched sound.

A double bass makes lower-pitched sounds than a whistle. The vibrations it makes are slower so it produces fewer vibrations in a second and a low sound.

With a partner, discuss sound sources that make high and low sounds.

1a List three sound sources that produce high sounds.

1b List three sound sources that produce low sounds.

Exploring Changing Pitch

Different musical instruments have different frequencies of vibrations, so make sounds of different pitches. We bang, shake, pluck or blow instruments to create vibrations and make sounds.

High and low sounds

You will need: instruments similar to those in the picture

1 Work in a small group. Play the instruments and discuss the pitches of the sounds they produce.

2a Classify the instruments into those that make a high sound, those that make a low sound and those that can make sounds at various pitches.

2b Record your findings on a Venn diagram.

3 Name another instrument that could be added to each group.

Investigate it!

We can make our own instruments that can make sounds at different pitches using everyday objects. High-pitched sounds are short, fast (high-frequency) vibrations. Low-pitched sounds are longer, slower vibrations (low-frequency).

Making instruments

You will need: a set of baby stacking cups (or plastic food boxes of different sizes without lids), rubber bands of different lengths and thicknesses

Work in a small group.

1a Explore making sounds by stretching the same size of elastic band over the different-sized stacking cups and plucking the band.

1b How does the pitch differ over the different-sized cups? Why?

2 Predict how changing the thickness of the band changes the pitch of the sound.

3 How could you carry out an investigation to find out whether changing the thickness of the band changes the pitch of the sound?

4 Investigate to test your predictions. Discuss your results.

Oboe straws

You will need: plastic drinking straws, a pair of scissors

1 Squash and cut the end of the straw like the one in the diagram.

2 Place the straw about 2 cm into your mouth and close your lips around the straw.

3 Blow until you make a sound.

4 How do you think you can make oboe straws that make sounds at different pitches? Test to find out.

5a How did the pitch change with length of the oboe straw?

5b Why did it change in this way?

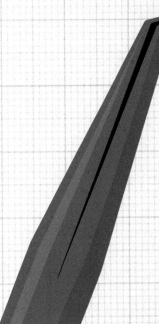

Measuring the Volume of Sounds

Sounds can be loud or quiet. The loudness of a sound is measured in **decibels** (dB). We call how loud a sound is its volume.

Word box
decibels

Large vibrations make loud sounds. Small vibrations make quieter sounds. The vibrations of this pneumatic drill produce sounds that are loud enough to damage human hearing. Workers in very loud environments need sound-absorbing ear defenders to protect their hearing.

Changing the volume of sounds

You will need a variety of different types of instruments, like the ones on page 11.

1 Play the instruments. Explore how to make loud and quiet sounds with the instruments.

📄 2 How did you change the volume of the sound?

📄 1 How is the sound volume different around your school? Use a data logger to measure volume in different places and compare the volumes.

Far Away Sounds – Plan it!

Have you ever waited for a train? Sometimes you can hear a train approaching a station before you see it.

1 What happens to the sound of a train as it gets closer?

Some animals have huge ears that are very sensitive and collect a lot of sounds.

2 Do you think this fennec fox can hear sounds that are too far away for us to hear? Why?

Sometimes we are too far away to hear sounds. Some children say this is why they cannot hear the bell being rung at the end of play time.

3 In your group discuss how you could do an investigation to find out how far away you would need to be before you could not hear a small bell ringing.

4 Record how you would find out.

5 Carry out your investigation and record your results.

Glossary

Auditory nerve the nerve at the back of the ear that tells the brain what has been heard

Compression wave the type of wave that sound is

Decibels unit we use to measure how loud sounds are

Frequency number of sound vibrations in a second

High (sound) squeaky sound (like a mouse makes); high-pitched

Loud sound that is very easy to hear; if a sound is very loud it can hurt our ears

Low (sound) gruff sound (like a bear makes); low-pitched

Noise sound that can be unpleasant

Outer ear visible part of the ear on the side of our head

Phenomenon something we can observe happening but not observe *how* it is happening

Pitch how high or low a sound is

Quiet sound that is not easy to hear

Source (sound) the thing that makes the sound

Vibrating moving backwards and forwards very quickly

Volume how quiet or loud a sound is